Shout Outs

Debra Trappen and
Fire Up! Taking Your Life and Business to 11...

"Debra is 100% authentic - she lives and breathes her personal brand and her story. She isn't a speaker or writer who talks about one thing and does another. She truly walks the walk. She is also one of the kindest people I know but is also completely straight-forward and will tell you like it is - to bring out your personal best!"

- Katie Lance
Founder & Social Media Strategist, Katie Lance Consulting

"Debra is one of the few people I can go to when I am in a funk or need advice and immediately feel like I can accomplish anything. There are so many influencers that are not positive or humble and that is what Debra personifies. I am blessed to call her a friend and a mentor. She is a "what you see is what you get" gal and that is so needed in today's business world."

- Lisa Archer
CEO Live Love Homes & Co-Founder of The Geeky Girls

"Debra's delivery technique begins with her own highly recognizable personal brand at D11. Right from get go of her FIRE UP presentations she sets the tone. Her message is truly one of authenticity, relevancy, competency with a twist of transparency for her audience and this creates attention & engagement factor needed to retain the content shared."

- Virginia Munden
CEO/Founder of Virginia Munden - Business & RE Coach

"I'm a creator. When my mind gets going it is difficult to daisy chain the ideas and make sure I am not going off on a tangent. Debra has been an incredible barometer. She has the uncanny ability of looking through all the madness and pulling the gems out and assisting with the framework. It's the wind beneath my wings when it comes to ideas and getting everything pulled together.

Most entrepreneurs' biggest challenge is getting the ideas in an executable position. Debra is excellent at making it a winning process. It's actually helped me take my ideas to the next level so I can make them a reality."

- Kelly Mitchell
Founder, Agent Caffeine and CoFounder, Women on Wine TV

"Debra has a way of making you sit back and focus on yourself. Focus to the point that you see things more clearly in your mind. Then, with her core values, you are able to focus on what you need to do and clearly think without the distractions of everyday life."

- Robert Stern
Founder, The Social Leade

Fire Up!

Taking Your Life
and Business to 11…

Jill –
Thank you
for all you do to
serve and inspire
the industry.
Enjoy your
Fire Up journey!

By Debra Trappen

Foreword by Rebekah Radice

Published by e5 publishing
Copyright © 2015 by Debra Trappen

Book Cover Designed By:
bccreativemedia.com

Interior Formatting By:
BestBookWriter.com

ISBN 978-0-9961194-0-5

CONTENTS

This book is dedicated to my bold, supportive and loving husband, Andrew.

Along the way, his servant heart, patience, and genuine, deep love have lifted me up, inspired me and grounded me.

Special thanks to my Pops and Queen Mum... Being raised by an engineer with a passion for sci-fi and a power women entrepreneur with grace and passion for others has shaped me into the woman I am today.

I am forever grateful for the love and support that surrounds me.

FOREWORD

When Debra Trappen asked me to write the foreword to her book, "Fired Up! Taking Your Life and Business to 11...," I was thrilled. Having known Debra both offline and online for several years, I know what a remarkable woman she is.

Our first introduction was through social media. It wasn't until some time after that when we finally met face to face. I remember it as if it were yesterday. I walked into an opening night cocktail party at the Inman Connect Real Estate Conference in San Francisco. There, in the middle of the room, surrounded by at least a dozen women was Debra.

I quickly crossed the room and snuck in a hello, not wanting to interrupt the hubbub that her presence had inspired. After our initial greeting, which more than likely included a hug and many squeals of delight, I listened in as Debra mesmerized her crowd of adoring fans.

Now when I say mesmerize, certainly it could be over her beauty. Whether you know Debra online or off, you can't help but notice her stunning good looks. Who could miss that fiery red hair? Her hair seemingly puts the spark in her spunky and always memorable banter.

Debra is so much more than that. She captivates the crowd because of her ability to speak to the very core of what makes us all tick. So while she's beautiful, she's also brilliant, charming, charismatic and extremely knowledgeable when it comes to fusing passion with human communication.

Debra has an innate capacity to take any situation and turn it into a moment. And making the most of each and every moment is the very essence of Debra's life mission. Her teaching is practical and actionable, giving you the tools you need to not just live life, but also give flight to a life you have only seen in your dreams.

This book contains everything you need to stop dreaming and start doing, to stop surviving and start thriving. Every section of this book contains proven steps and strategies that Debra has used to help others get from where they are, to where they want to be. Her book is a testament to her years of work identifying what holds us back in life and how to shed those limiting beliefs and step into a positive, productive and profitable mindset.

Now, let me warn you. If you're looking for coddling, handholding or someone to tell you that staying in your comfort zone is ok, you have come to the wrong place. You're also not going to find any fluffy anecdotes or convoluted theories. Debra's a straightforward, tell it like it is, no-nonsense gal. Her approach is a breath of fresh air and one that has resonated deeply with me since the day I met her.

My hope is that you'll gain as much from this book as I have. That you'll walk away inspired and empowered to make the necessary changes within your own life and business. I know that through Debra's skilled instruction, you will be able to push through the tough stuff, the not so fun stuff, but the stuff we all have to work through to truly know success, no matter what that looks like to you.

I know that if you commit to following the book through, from beginning to end, you will come out on the other side having uncovered a whole new you!

Rebekah Radice
Social Media Strategist | Award Winning Blogger
Rebekah Radice, LLC

PEEK BEHIND THE SCENES

What does "Take It To 11" mean?
Why #FireMeUp11?
What's up with the number 11?

People often ask me these questions... and I love it. The number 11 is part of my story and sharing "why" always ignites me. So, here it goes:

My love of 11 went to an 11 when I met my amazing husband. I was living in apartment #1111 – he was living in #11. We were engaged on 11/11, married on an 11th and celebrate every 11th - every month. When we see 11:11 it reminds us to slow down and connect to one another, and count our blessings.

Friends and family – both online and off – associate the number 11 with me. Friends from all around the world send screenshots of their phone at 11:11, when they are sitting at table 11, when they are at exit 11 - you get the idea. It has become my "Social Object", that "thing" outside of a logo, name, or photo that reminds people of me. (Do you have a social object?)

In my life and business, the number 11 is a reminder to stop, think about what is happening in that moment, and challenge myself to take the EXPERIENCE to the next level. Add a little extra "something" to make what I'm preparing, creating, or engaging in even more remarkable, memorable and even truly unforgettable.

This book is all about guiding you through the process to taking your brand, business and LIFE to an 11, too! My heart's desire is to inspire you to ask yourself:

- **What one thing can I do today to "Take It To 11"?**
- **Why settle for a TEN when I can go to 11?**

What is a #MoxieMemo?

You will also notice me sharing something called a **#MoxieMemo**. These are short, succinct quotes or truths to **FIRE YOU UP**, get you out of your own way so you start living your best life and embracing your greatest potential!

My personal brand/passion statement shines a light on the core of my life's work, so far:

"To ignite passion, infuse purpose, and inspire progress by connecting, engaging, elevating and empowering the

magnificent relationships and brilliant ideas in my world."

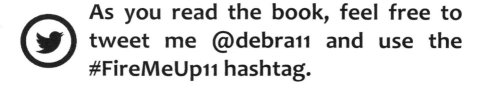

As you read the book, feel free to tweet me @debra11 and use the #FireMeUp11 hashtag.

If you are inspired to share a #moxiememo please include that tag too!

I look forward to engaging with you, whether at one of my workshops, an education/speaking event or in the social media streams.

What is Personal Brand? ... a specific image or impression – about YOU – in the minds of others!

~ Debra Trappen

d11consulting.com

INTRODUCTION

Let's be real. For most people, some of the biggest challenges with "personal brand" are simply understanding what it is... why they need it... and how they build one. Let's start by tackling these three questions.

What Is Personal Brand?

Personal brand, if you will, is a specific image or impression in the mind of others about YOU.

It is the words people use to describe you; the things that remind them of you and the way you make them feel. It may include words, topics, attitude, colors, numbers, clothing, etc. that trigger YOU in their mind - these are elements of your "personal brand".

The elements of YOU!

Why Do You Need It?

First of all, let's be clear - you already have a personal brand, so it is less about "why" you need it and more about embracing your responsibility (and gift) to define and nurture it.

A strong personal brand can be the difference between mediocre success and extraordinary success - both in life and business. It doesn't matter if you are an entrepreneur marketing your professional services or ideas; an intrapreneur looking for a new job or career; or simply an individual with a desire to build your industry influence, the size/focus of your sphere, or credibility online - **you are marketing yourself** so those people you want to connect with can FIND YOU.

Do you know the answers to these questions?

- What am I doing to inspire others to read and listen to my messages or use my products and services?
- How do I convince them I am right for a project?
- How am I the best resource for them - what is my relevant, valuable offering?

Personal Branding is Authentically YOU.   Personal Branding Is REAL.

It's your opportunity to share your vision of who you are and what you uniquely have to offer. If you don't define and share your personal brand story, you are allowing others to determine what you are all about, what you do, why you do it, and ultimately share their version. This is a risk you can easily avoid, so let's get to it!

How do you build your personal brand?

Designing a strong **personal brand foundation** starts with focusing in on your "Core Four":

1. **Personal Core Values**
2. **Soul Tank Fuel (aka Passions)**
3. **Your Life's Purpose – Your WHY!**
4. **Niche Statement**

You are defining and nurturing who you are, who your ideal clients/connections are, and how you are the solution to their problems. Once you clarify, and consistently share your personal brand Core Four, you start to build influence and a connection with those people you are equipped to and desire to serve.

In other words, a solid personal brand will attract the ideal people, opportunities and success to you - like a magnet.

Success – whatever that means to you - is sitting on the other side of your comfort zone.

- **Are you ready to move towards that success and start your personal brand journey?**

- **Are you ready to get uncomfortable to become unstoppable?**

The next several chapters include a deep dive into each of the Core Four to get you on the path to a clear, concise personal brand foundation that you are confident about – from the inside out!

I believe you are ready... and I dare you to believe it too!

Chapter 1

Defining Your Core Values

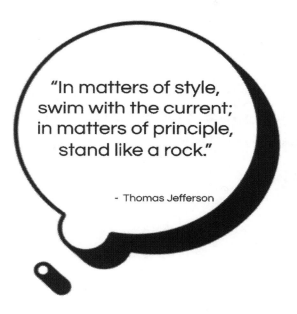

"In matters of style, swim with the current; in matters of principle, stand like a rock."

- Thomas Jefferson

The first element in your Core Four is your list of core values! It's time to put your 5-point harness on and get this journey started by defining your core values - also known as your personal principles!

I truly believe stating your core values is like embracing a SUPER POWER.

When you value something, people recognize it. People see and believe it. Passion and enthusiasm may open the door, however a clear vision and defined values will fascinate your audience and inspire them to build a relationship and partnership with you. Solid values attract clients who share the same mindset as you do... and are essential to your personal brand.

Are you living your values or are your choices forcing you to live out of alignment?

Do you find yourself making statements that SCREAM you are living outside your values?

Statements like:

"I haven't had time to meet up with and connect with loved ones in weeks."
(Values Out of Alignment: Relationships, Connection, Family or Friends)

"Workout or sit down to eat? When? I don't have time!"
(VOA: Healthy Living/Fitness/Time Blocking)

"I can't remember the last time I had a moment to myself."
(VOA: Alone Time/Introspection/Tranquility/Awareness)

"My schedule is so crazy. I haven't seen my children or tucked them in for days!"
(VOA: Family/Children)

"My house is in chaos - the dishes and laundry are piling up as I speak!"
(VOA: Aesthetics/Excellence/Organization/Cleanliness)

"I haven't been on a vacation forever."
(VOA: Adventure/Fun/Downtime)

If you are nodding your head thinking – YES, I have said some of those things (or a lot of them) you are NOT alone.

Shame. OFF. You.

NOW is the time to stop. Reevaluate. Re-prioritize. It's time to finally GET REAL.

The truth is "Defining Your Values 101" is not part of the general curriculum in school. No one spells it out or helps you outline what you really want when you grow up. Most of us become who we are due to circumstance. We graduate, jump into a career, marriage, family and then, one day, wake up feeling off – way off. Oodles of people talk about "values". They remind you to live by them and run your businesses by them, but how do you really know WHAT yours are. I say it's time to discover!

This all sounds good – but really, why should you go through all of it? You know it is not going to be an easy task, so what could possibly be worth it?

Well, I believe when you fully understand and operate from your values...

MAGIC happens.

Most noticeably, at least for my clients and me –> decisions get clearer. You don't need to flip coins to choose your options. You now have a list of values that assist you in YOUR choices. Imagine your values as your internal compass to keep you aligned and present in your life.

Step 1: Define Your Values.

What are your top 11 values? It is hard to intentionally live by them if you don't know what they are or have not written them down. There are many ways you can go through this process. The end result is the same. There is a modified values exercise in the back of this book. There is also a more robust version here: firemeup11.com/ValuesExercise

Step 2: Practice the P.A.C.E. process!

Before you say YES to an invitation to have coffee, become a volunteer, partner on a new project, plan or attend an event, review these steps:

Pause: Take a moment to answer any request.

Assess: Ask yourself: "Does this opportunity align with my values?"

Choose: You now have the option to choose wisely. Not every single decision you make will fit perfectly into your value structure, but when you use this process you are consciously aware - from the start.

Execute: Now you can confidently and intentionally, integrate the activity, nurture the relationship, etc. knowing it will add value to your life – in alignment with your core principles.

Doesn't that sound amazing?

Here are some examples:

YOU VALUE: Positivity

- **REVIEW INVITATIONS TO SHARE TIME TOGETHER:**
Does she consistently bring positive energy to the conversation, talk about how she is overcoming/embracing a business challenge and thrive on sharing her connections to build strong businesses - together? OR... Are you coming home from your coffee connect with a sour attitude because "Mr. Toxic" just spent an hour complaining about his life, marriage, job, etc?

YOU VALUE: Healthy Living

- **SHOPPING:**
Do the stores I shop in align with my values, either by philosophy, ingredients or experience standards? Are the items in my basket going to get me closer to my health goals or the meal plans I have designed for my family?

- **EVENING HABITS:**
If you want to add in meditation, yoga, exercise,

writing, reading, or even more sleep – look closely at your evening commitments. Do they align? Can you move a couple dinner meetings to breakfast, lunch or an afternoon coffee chat?

- **SCHEDULING MEETINGS:**
  Be conscious of where you are holding your meetings. Can you switch food centric or happy hour meetings to "walking meetings"? (Perhaps these walks will also help with a "financial freedom" value too!)

An additional, FANTASTIC bonus to getting clear about your values is you will get more confident and comfortable saying **NO**!

"No."

The word "no" is actually a complete sentence.

Are you ready to define your values and embrace your super powers now?

#moxiememo

"Stating your values is like embracing a SUPER POWER!"

Chapter 2

Fueling Your Soul Tank

"Passion is energy.
Feel the power
that comes from
focusing on what
excites you."

- Oprah Winfrey

The second element in your Core Four is to get in touch with what you are truly passionate about – right now.

- What activities FIRE YOU UP and fill your soul tank?
- What makes you smile, relax, laugh, sing, shout or dance uncontrollably?
- What **PASSION CULTURE** do you want to inspire in your life?

The "soul tank" element of your Core Four is about defining and infusing those activities and things into your life. This list will also be a key element in attracting ideal connections – whether they are personal or business relationships.

Knowing what ignites a spark inside you or elevates your mood seems simple. However many people don't slow down long enough to think about these things – let alone define or infuse them. If you don't recognize and infuse what you have genuine passion for in your life, you will never fully convince or inspire people to partner with you or join your movement.

Let's start some simple questions:

- What do you do for fun?

- Do you have a charity you love to share?

- Do you have a divine passion for wine, yoga, dogs, cats, hiking or organic essential oils?

- Maybe you collect vintage vehicles, vinyl records, or typewriters?

If you aren't sure WHAT you are passionate about or how to define it, no worries - that is why we are doing this together now.

It's never too late to design a SOUL TANK MENU, so let's get started!

Step 1: Complete a Passions Exercise

The goal here is to write a list of 11+ things that fill your soul tank, make you laugh, and generally FIRE YOU UP!

If you want or need a bit more assistance or some deeper inspiration, feel free to download a free exercise here: firemeup11.com/PassionsExercise

Remember, the items on your list should be things you are or can do right now. They can be free activities, types of conversations, things you love to create, etc. The thought of them brings a smile to your face and ignites a spark inside.

Your passions are those things or activities that FIRE YOU UP and fuel your soul tank!

#MoxieMemo: Have some FUN with your list and create a Pinterest pin board that represents your passion list. When you are feeling like you could use a mindset shift – you can visit your board for a quick attitude BOOST!

It is important not to mistake the things you DREAM of doing as your "passions". Once accomplished, they may become passions but until then, those belong on your bucket list.

Step 2: INFUSE Your Passions

Once you have defined your soul tank menu it is time to INFUSE those things into your daily life.

Take some time each week to schedule in your PASSION time... you can always squeeze in a 2-minute-puppy-belly-rubbing-session or a 30 second dance party on those days when you just don't "have time"! The people in your life will thank you for taking the time, and so will your soul.

Having a hard time with doing this with consistency? Try partnering up with a friend and keeping each other accountable. It takes weeks to form a new habit, so give yourself grace and set yourself up for success.

 #MoxieMemo: Create a recurring monthly or quarterly reminder to revisit your list. Add in new passions and remove those you are no longer interested in pursuing. A fresh, ever-changing list (or pin board) is an ACTIVE one!

Step 3: Make Informed Choices Using Your List

Sofia is an entrepreneur AND has a passion for wine. During our sessions together, we put together a plan to infuse "wine" into her business and attract clients who share a similar passion. We reviewed these areas:

- Where could she host her next client event?
  -> A local winery for a wine tasting event.

- What could her clients appreciation gifts be?
  -> A bottle of her favorite wine or personal blend.

- Where could she network to meet new clients?

-> Winery or wine bar events: vertical wine tastings, live music, cheese pairings or one of those fun "wine & painting" events.

Many of these are also be in alignment with her values: creativity, knowledge, relationships and adventure.

Are you starting to see the difference it makes when you have both your values and passions defined and infused into your life plan?

Have you started to dream up ways you can put your first two lists together to FIRE UP your life and business?

 I would love to know what you are cooking up... Don't forget to tweet me @debra11 and use the #FireMeUp11 hashtag to share!

All right, are you ready for the third phase in the "Core Four journey"?

It is time to TURN YOUR PURPOSE ON!

Chapter 3

Discovering Your Purpose

"Be yourself; everyone else is taken!"

- Oscar Wilde

Your purpose (aka "your WHY") is constantly empowering you. Your life-purpose is something you do so effortlessly and naturally, you have probably overlooked it for many years. It is likely inspiring you to learn and grow. Your why is so simple that it fires you up and into your magnificence when are on the right path. You can feel it when you find it. **It feels right.**

Nearly every single day I have a conversation with a friend, client, or audience member that ends in the question "What is your WHY?"

Ooooodles of questions arise, like:

Q1. Do I need to know what my purpose is?
Q2. Why does a "why statement" matter?
Q3. Seriously, is it possible to really define my why?

My answers typically sound something like this:

A1. "You don't need a WHY statement to live; however I believe defining it equips you to live a life with focus and intentionally leverage your true purpose. "
A2. "It matters because it creates clarity... and a deeper understanding of who you are."
A3. "Yes, it is truly possible to define your why."

#MoxieMemo: There is no magic pill formula to define your why. You have creative freedom, flexibility, and time to write, revise, and refine it... as long as it takes to get you there.

It is also important to realize that the journey doesn't end once your define your why. Conscious living actually begins at that moment. You will be working to live by and engage it personally and professionally every day.

Are you ready?

To get you rolling, and hopefully inspire you, let me share my "why", as well as my personal purpose statement.

My why can be simplified to just a few words:
I FIRE PEOPLE UP.

(Sure, you could also say: I get people "unstuck", help people find clarity in chaos, shift their mindset, inspire them to take things to an 11 with many ideas and straight-talk... but the end result of all of these is feeling FIRED UP.)

My personal *purpose statement* adds a little sass and moxie and makes it my own:

"To ignite passion, infuse purpose, and inspire progress by connecting, engaging, elevating and empowering the magnificent relationships and brilliant ideas in my world."

I wrote this in 2002. Every single time I read this it fires ME up. Yours should too.

Let's get going on defining your WHY.

Step 1: LISTEN

Why?   People are likely already telling you your purpose!

"Thank you, (insert your name)! You are so good at (fill in the blank)!

The blanks might be:

- Teaching me something new when I see you

- Comforting me in my time of need

- Telling me just what I need to hear – whether I like it or not

- Making me laugh and reminding me to have fun...

Step 2: Uncovering Your Purpose Exercise

I encourage you to slow down to respect and honor the process of discovering your purpose. Schedule time when you can unwind. Pour yourself a cup of coffee, tea, or a velvety glass of wine, find a quiet spot and explore your purpose. My clients go through an 11-step process to define their purpose. To get you started, here are five questions:

Q1. What conversations set my soul on fire?

Q2. What activities do I get lost in where I lose track of time?

Q3. What do people typically ask me for help in?

Q4. If I could only share/teach one message to one group of people... what would my message be and whom would those people be?

Q5. If I knew I would never fail, what would I do, be or have?

Remember don't rush through this process.... However, don't spend too much time laboring over each step either. Trust yourself.

Write down the answers that immediately come to mind.

Want to dig even deeper?
Visit firemeup11.com/PurposeExercise for additional questions and exercises.

Ultimately, living your life with purpose and defining and embracing your WHY, will allow you to truly focus on things that matter most.

Don't worry if you are having a hard time "seeing" your purpose in your every day activities. However, before you go for a full "reinvention", stop and look at what you are doing now. If you believe you are not in the ideal job, you may be able to find greater purpose through **how you do what you do** right now, experience more fulfillment in and from it, and pour your greatness into your world as you look for your next step! You may not even realize how close you are to living out your purpose.

Most importantly, please don't give up. Push through the (unavoidable) moments of frustration during this process of discovery.

Our lives are designed to be overflowing with lessons and challenges. When you find yourself stuck on a question or exercise, try focusing on what answers ARE clear. Revel in those successes. Celebrate the clarity in those moments.

Discovery will come if you are willing to push through and take your tenacious spirit to an 11!

Be Fearless. Be Fierce.
Let people call you crazy.
Dream BIG.
TAKE ACTION
Embrace who YOU are.
Become your BEST SELF.

@debra11 * d11consulting * #FireMeUp11

Chapter 4

Creating Your Niche

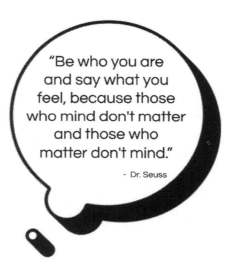

"Be who you are and say what you feel, because those who mind don't matter and those who matter don't mind."

— Dr. Seuss

Our final Core Four element is all about discovering and formulating YOUR niche... then SHARING it with people!

Too many entrepreneurs and intrapreneurs (an inside entrepreneur, or an entrepreneur within a large firm, who uses entrepreneurial skills without incurring the risks associated with those activities) start out believing they can or should be all things to all people.

They believe they are "leaving business on the table" when they focus on a target market.

However, businesses owners taking on this EVERYTHING attitude risk many issues including burnout, exhaustion, confusion, and failure. By defining a specific niche (a well-defined segment of a larger market), you - the business owner - know what message/experience to deliver; your customers know exactly what to expect; and your sphere of champions knows how to share your message with others!

Since it is difficult to be all things to all people, you must craft niches to suit your business needs and resources. Creating your niche will give your business (or career, if you are an intrapreneur) the greatest chance of success, but where do you start?

Simply put —> **DEFINE IT**.

Here are 5 key ways to get you on the path to defining your niche:

1. DEFINE YOUR IDEAL CUSTOMER

Get focused... this is who you are going to work with every day. What type of lifestyle does your target audience live? How old are they? What are they passionate about doing, solving, or being?

Rather than choosing a broad category, narrow your target customer down, think about things like: gender, geographical location, married or single, hobbies, employer or occupation, etc. When you define your ideal customer you are also defining the language you use, pin pointing the platforms you use to engage and promote on, and allowing yourself to focus in and learn all you can about that specific demographic.

BONUS: All of these help in strengthening your brand as "The GO TO" in the niche.

2. PICK AN INDUSTRY TO SERVE

Start by asking yourself some questions to help you choose:

What industries do you know? What industries do you love? What industries do you have influence in? Is there one industry that is the answer to all three questions? If so, start there!

Remember, it is important to have a passion for what you do AND for those you serve. As an entrepreneur, you get to choose – so choose wisely. You might know a ton about the wine industry and you may have influence in it, but if you don't get up every single day with an electric attitude to make, taste, and sell more wine...

Well, you get the idea!

3. SPECIALIZE IN A SPECIFIC SERVICE OR PRODUCT

Many small businesses make a big mistake here, and try to offer every type of service or product they can for their market. Remember, the concept is being known for a specialty. For instance, saying "I sell real estate in Seattle" is just too broad. "I sell bungalows (or condos or multi-unit buildings) in the Capitol Hill area" is specific. When you state your specialty, people are able to catalogue it and can refer you business much easier.

4. LOOK FOR AN IGNORED OR FORGOTTEN AUDIENCE

There are always groups of people who have specific conditions or needs that automatically make it difficult to find service providers. Maybe a "generalization" has caused your competitors to label a specific generation "not interesting yet". **When this group of people find out THEY are your specialty,** you will have secured clients for life. If you market well and provide them a platform to share the story of your business, they will also help you build your business with referrals.

5. BE IN THE KNOW

There are many ways to find out trends in your niche of choice. Get rolling with these:

- Search it out online! If you want to start selling personal training services, do a quick online search to find out how many others are in this space in your area. This quick snapshot will teach you a lot about the industry you are interested in, how others are marketing themselves, and possibly even show a gap in the space.
- Set up a RSS Feed or Lists to keep up on top industry blogs and bloggers.
- Work the hashtag searches... and LISTEN on social media platforms! Over a billion people are on Facebook alone, so social can no longer be ignored. It provides insight into what your

target demographics wants and loves – for FREE. Join a G+ Community or LinkedIn Group... set up listening lists on Twitter... If your business matches the Instagram platform/ demographic – make sure you are searching for top hashtags around your niche – and use them!

Last, but not least:

FORMULATE YOUR NICHE STATEMENT

An ideal niche statement formula looks like this:

audience + problem + solution + promise = success

Start by writing down these four elements:

1. Your ideal client/audience (I work with _____)
2. Their problem (who want/need to _____)
3. Your solution (If you are ready to or it is time to _____)
4. Your promise (I will _____)

Here is one of my client's mission and niche statements, as an example:

Our mission as a marketing and speaker talent agency is to inspire and cultivate success in the hearts and minds of audiences around the world by providing captivating speakers and creative marketing strategies that drive action and results.

We are in pursuit of **passionate** speakers, leaders, entrepreneurs, innovators, and visionaries who think outside the box, follow a **purpose**, and take risks to achieve **greatness**. We serve event and marketing professionals who want to **influence** their companies, communities, industry events, sales organizations and consumers around the world. We don't overlook the small details as they can make the largest **impact**.

Vanessa Murray, TAKE Success, LLC

Here is another example:

"I work with entrepreneurs and small businesses who want to leverage social media to achieve their goals; (niche) those who know they need a strategy and have no idea where to begin (problem). If you are looking to build your business, find a new job, or build your sphere of influence (solution), I can help you clarify your story, define what social media platforms would be best for you to share it on, identify your target niche, and achieve your goals (promise)."

Are you ready to set your business and career up for success?

Work through these 5 keys and create your formula. This will help you get clarity.

If you prefer to download a complete niche statement exercise - visit my site: firemeup11.com/niche!

 #MoxieMemo: Now it is time to boldly go out there, get the attention of your target audience and ROCK YOUR VISION!

Chapter 5

Being Your Signature Self

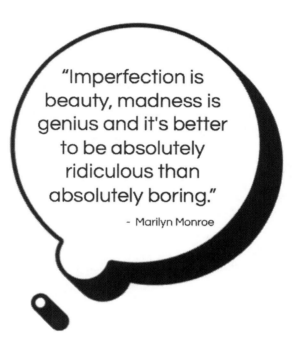

"Imperfection is beauty, madness is genius and it's better to be absolutely ridiculous than absolutely boring."

- Marilyn Monroe

Now that you have your Core Four defined and a strong personal brand foundation/message to share, it is time get comfortable in this new skin. Let's start with the basics of infusing your Core Four while being your signature self – both online and offline.

You know the world is full of knock-offs, spinoffs, and cheap imitations. You realize being "genuine" seems all to often to be the exception, not the norm. You know there is only ONE person just like you, so why do you fight being "yourself"?

I believe it all starts with LOVING yourself. Which leads me to the first tip.

Tip #1: Stop the negative self-talk.

You speak encouraging words to and believe in the greatness of others in your life. Where is the grace for you in all of this? What makes you and me always want to "be (or compare ourselves to) someone else"?

Well, for one, you likely don't "talk to yourself" like you talk to friends. You can be downright MEAN to yourself... calling yourself stupid, fat, ugly... not worthy. With all of those adjectives floating around your head – it is no wonder you don't embrace, elevate or empower yourself. You can understand how this would seriously get in the way of a healthy personal brand foundation!

Want to combat this?

Pretend you are talking to your 7-year-old self!

Would you say those things to her/him? I didn't think so. Whenever you are formulating "negative self talk" in your mind – stop and picture yourself with those piggy tails or in those Wonder Woman or Spiderman Underoos that made you feel like you could conquer the world. Now try saying those negative words to your mini you. It is crazy how well this works!

Enough is enough. It is time to acknowledge your greatness, embrace your distinctive combination of values, passions and purpose, and get excited that you really do have our own path.

Start believing there isn't anyone like you.

Accept your responsibility to be the best version of YOURSELF as possible!

What do you have to be afraid of here? Could it be:

- Your relationships might improve?
- Your businesses will flourish?

- Your consistent, day-to-day emotion could be HAPPINESS?

Come on now. You deserve happiness, love, and success.

REPEAT THIS AFTER ME:

"I deserve happiness, love, and success."

(Go on, I will wait.)

Now, **SAY IT AGAIN.** This time, stand up, put your hands in the air and **SHOUT IT OUT.**

"I deserve happiness, love, and success."

My dear reader, you deserve to live the purpose you were born to fulfill. *If you didn't try shouting it out while standing up "with your hands in the air like you just don't care"... you only cheated yourself. The rest of us have HUGE smiles on our faces!*

Know this: The world needs to be blessed by your talents - YOUR special gifts.

For this all to happen, you have to get over your negative thoughts, believe in yourself and start sharing your best self with the world! Need some help?

Here are 11 Affirmations to start infusing into your "self talk" time:

1. Loving myself is fabulously essential to my happiness and positive attitude.
2. I deserve to passionately go after my goals and do what makes my soul sizzle.
3. Accepting myself unconditionally gives me the power to succeed and rock my purpose.
4. I am an amazing person who deserves happiness, success, and love.
5. I accept myself deeply and completely.
6. I have limitless confidence in my talents and abilities.
7. Others will be inspired by my courage to be myself.
8. I will take time to recognize and celebrate my achievements.
9. I look forward to discovering new layers of myself every single day.
10. There is no one like me and I can't wait to share my talents today.
11. I am divine, complete and totally equipped to live my life and purpose out loud!

TIP 2: Stop comparing yourself to other people. NOW!

Battling or embracing your self-doubt and focusing on "the competition" are some of the top ways we keep ourselves from achieving GREATNESS.

If you are waging war against yourself... STOP. Remember, there is NO ONE like you. You are in competition with no one.

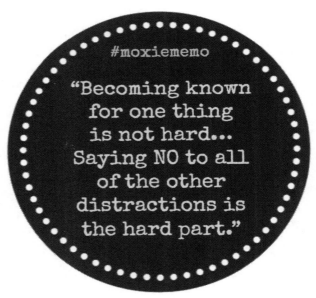

#moxiememo

"Becoming known
for one thing
is not hard...
Saying NO to all
of the other
distractions is
the hard part."

Reset your mind and focus on your passions, your purpose, your values... those things that make you uniquely YOU. Bring THOSE to the table today. Spread your sparkle... Sprinkle your glitter... Get out there and SHINE.

Being your SIGNATURE SELF is your responsibility. No one else can do it for you. You focusing on what everyone else is doing is only keeping YOU from your greatness. It doesn't slow them down one bit...

Here are 5 "Mindset Shift Tips/Tricks" to try when fighting these battles:

1. Call a friend. The REAL one who doesn't whisper fluffy kitten talk in your ear, but gives it to you STRAIGHT, kicks you in the toosh when you need it, and reminds you of your greatness.

2. Take a walk. Leave your phone at home. Enjoy the fresh air and reconnect with the life sounds around you. If you have a dog, bring them along. They are fabulous partners and have been known to listen (and solve) many problems.

3. Close the curtains. Light some candles. Indulge in a bubble bath - in the middle of the day. Yep. INDULGE. Don't judge. Try it. It works. Not into bubble baths – substitute your own "me time" activity!

4. Crank the music up and have a personal dance party. Pity parties are just plain lame. Dance parties fill your soul tank.

5. Kick into a Stretch * Meditate * Prayer Session... I find that when I slow down, stretch, and get back to my true center - I return with a CHAMPION attitude.

Take a moment and write down what YOU do to renew and refocus your mind when those irritating self-doubt thoughts start whispering in your ear.

 Feeling bold and daring? Share them with me on Twitter using the hashtag #FireMeUp11 and tag me @debra11.

Now, I am going to get on my sassy redhead soapbox and recap, so put your listening ears and seatbelts on...

#moxiememo

When you embrace your authentic self... You have NO competition!

~ Debra Trappen

YOU were born an original...

Don't live like a copy.

Find your voice.

Embrace your uniqueness.

YOU are here for a purpose.

No one else can do what YOU do how you do it. Period.

Stop focusing on what others are doing or saying.

It is a waste of your time.

Get comfortable in your skin.

Be intentional with your choice to be your BEST YOU every day.

Sparkle. Shine. Inspire.

B-R-E-A-T-H-E and SMILE!

You have invested precious time into designing a solid personal brand foundation. It is your turn to knock out self-doubt and embrace your brilliant, signature self!

#moxiememo

You were born an
ORIGINAL.
Don't live like a copy.
Find your VOICE.
EMBRACE your uniqueness.

Sparkle. Shine. Sizzle.

~ Debra Trappen

dllconsulting.com

Chapter 6

Fun Ways To Share Your Story

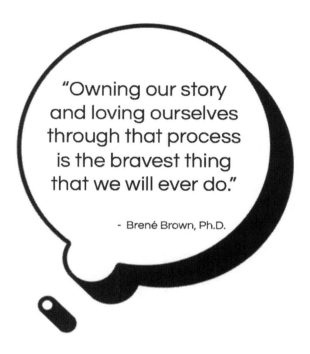

"Owning our story
and loving ourselves
through that process
is the bravest thing
that we will ever do."

- Brené Brown, Ph.D.

Now that you have your Core Four elements defined and a healthy attitude adjustment on embracing your magnificence - your personal brand is ready for the "unveiling party" online! A strong personal brand (like yours!) weaves and tells a powerful, memorable, and believable story. Stories inspire.

When you are able to INSPIRE your audience you are, in essence, sharing and selling yourself at the same time. You create a connection to your vision, values, and passions by LIVING your signature brand "story".

Let's talk about the top two tips to leverage and share your Core Four story online:

Tip #1: VISUAL STORYTELLING

One of the simplest ways to share your Core Four online is by visually telling your story. Using photos and videos, also increases your engagement – especially over plain text posts.

It is time to pull out your values and passions list WORDS and put them into action online. While sharing your love of hiking, wine, dogs, or yoga can be easily shared with a few words in a status update – adding some sizzle to your content with a photo or video takes it to an 11!

 #MoxieMemo: The more detailed, engaging and consistent your story is – the more memorable it is!

Need some inspiration or examples? Here are a couple of my clients:

> Liz is incredibly passionate about volunteering in her community. She regularly would post updates like "I am off to volunteer at a local shelter today!" Now, there is nothing wrong with the post. However, when she switched over to sharing photos from the exciting shelter project she was managing, her engagement increased tenfold!
>
> Why? Quite simply: she was sharing the story – her behind the scenes – with her friends and followers. They could SEE it and connect with it... and were inspired to ask questions about the work she was doing. A few people even got involved with her project!
>
> Susie is a passionate foodie and wine lover, however her career has nothing to do with either... or does it? Susie is a real estate professional. That means she serves and sells her community – a town filled with fabulous restaurants and a personal gourmet kitchen packed with cookbooks and homemade nibbles.

She was not sure how to share this in a relevant way, so we put together a simple strategy for her.

Instead of posting she is "cooking/baking today or perusing cookbooks" she now takes a photo of the delicious food she makes and shares it on Facebook. The engagement grows with each post. Not only is she sharing her personal passion for food and cooking – she is creating a deeper connection with other foodies and attracting new connections that are interested too!

Tip #2: BLOG. VLOG. PODCAST. OH MY!

Part of sharing your personal brand story is about engaging and attracting your ideal connections. In addition, the ability to influence and impact your world increases exponentially. In order to be recognized as a thought-leader or inspiration in your industry you must leverage your Core Four and SHARE YOUR THOUGHTS. Sounds simple, however so many people get caught up in excuses and never make it to the sharing piece.

You don't have to write a book to share your thoughts. Start with writing a blog post on your own website – once a week or even once/twice a month. If you don't have your own website, offer to guest post on a website that focuses on serving your niche or industry.

Weekly/monthly contributions introduce who you are to the world, they also show tenacity, consistency and that you are literate. If you don't have the time for writing in this current season of your life, there are options. A few of my clients have hired a trusted professional to write for them - in THEIR VOICE. There are ghostwriters who will take the time to get to know you, your style, and will provide custom posts for you. No more "canned" excuses. Take action and get it done! Remember, good, error-free content that shares you and shines a light on your brand is what you are seeking. Don't let the need to be perfect stand in the way of promoting your brand and sharing your story!

If you enjoy being in front of the camera, start a video blog. These do not have to be professional video quality! Use your laptop camera, a couple of well-placed lamps, and a quality external microphone to get started. You can be the solo star of your show sharing your perspectives, passions and purpose; you can interview others who service your niche/industry; or a fun combination of both.

If you don't want to be on camera, but still have something to say, start a podcast. There are plenty of great resources out there to get you started. Pop on over to Google or Bing and search "how do I start a podcast?" or "how do I start an online show?".

> A client and fabulous friend, Kelly Mitchell, runs an incredibly successful podcast. Her "why" behind the show: "stimulate, invigorate, and inspire ideas". She interviews industry innovators and influencers who are willing to "open their kimono" and share secrets to their success and lessons from their failures. She was getting tens of thousands of downloads every month... and it was continuing to grow at a normal pace. However, after doing her passions list – it was clear her love for acting was not being realized. After plenty of sassy encouragement she decided to incorporate a VIDEO interview with her podcast. Her desire to share the message of leaders was complimented by her talent to light up the screen.... voila! As a result of her passion being infused into her plan -

the show downloads, social media engagement, and audience have all increased at a rapid pace. She is also expanding her media company to include additional channels that will speak into other industries and audiences!

Fun tidbit: Kelly and I host a video show together called #WomenOnWine.TV. Real life insights and relevant guests are woven into our weekly conversation – always over a glass of divine wine. Topics are focused around building a business, branding, social media, and LIFE… always from a woman's perspective - for women and men who dare to understand us! Visit womenonwine.tv to learn more.

Finally, another easy way to share your thoughts is to curate excellent content from other authors that speak to your Core Four. What blogs are you already reading? If you are not following any blogs now, do a little research and start following the bloggers who resonate with you. Sign up to receive new posts in your inbox and/or follow them on Twitter. When their post evokes an emotion from you – share it on your social streams. The key is to ADD YOUR OWN THOUGHTS when you share it. Let other people know what you liked, what riled you up, or what you are going to try because of it.

 Have an idea for a podcast, but not sure how to implement? Tweet me @debra11 and tag #FireMeUp11!

Tip #3: HOST EVENTS

A FUN way to share your Core Four is putting together events that support and represent them! If you are passionate about dogs and wine – put together (or participate in) a walk-a-thon to raise funds for a local animal shelter.

One of my dearest clients, Carol Farrar of 1850 Realty, NAILS this concept with her Throwback Thursday events. Here is her story:

Carol values and has a true passion for 3 C's: community, collaboration and contribution. However, she wasn't sure how to put all of the pieces of the puzzle together. During one of our d11 #FireMeUp11 Sessions the two of us put together a strategic plan to infuse all of her C's and "Throwback Thursdays" were born! #TBT is monthly event that supports a local brewery (infusing her background in and love for craft beer) and brings awareness to a local charity while "throwing one back" with the local community. People love it! These monthly events fulfill her 3 C's, are highly attended, and have produced more recognition, for Carol and her team, as supporters of the community. It differentiates 1850 Realty from others in the San Diego area, attracts attention from others in the real estate industry AND she is having fun doing it!

Planning events and sparking conversations connected to your Core Four will not only be interesting to continue, but it will let your friends and followers know a bit more about you with each post.

 #MoxieMemo: Keeping your "story content" authentic and interesting makes it easier for clients to delight in the experience of following you, reading and sharing your posts, remembering key points, and sparking actions that builds deeper relationships and more business!

Chapter 7

Taking Your Story ONLINE

"Good content isn't about good storytelling. It's about telling a true story well."

- Ann Handley

I am often asked, "WHERE should I post online?" There are so many social media platforms out there... "How do I know which one is best for me?" There is a simple answer with a lengthy explanation... so here we go!

Step 1: KNOW WHAT YOU WANT TO ACCOMPLISH

The first thing you want to do is figure out what your top reasons for being online personally and professionally are.

Start by asking yourself these questions:

- Do I need to increase my visibility with a certain industry or influence group?
- Do I want to build credibility on a current passion or in a current or new industry?
- Am I seeking to secure new clients or personal connections?
- Do I want to build a community based on my passions?
- Am I looking to uncover new business opportunities?
- Am I ready for a new job or career?

Step 2: UNDERSTAND KEY PLATFORM USES

The following reviews the top platforms (as of Jan 2015) and tips and tricks on these elements by breaking them down.

- What is it? (A brief description of the platform)

- Ideas on what to share

- Who should you connect with there

- Who to connect with and why...

FACEBOOK PROFILE

What is it? An online platform to stay connected with friends and family, to discover what's going on in the world, and to share and express what matters to you.

Ideas on what to share: The moments of your life – mostly personal sprinkled with some professional. Photos, videos, blog posts, and quotes are the most frequent posts. Visuals tend to get much higher engagement.

Who should you connect with? People you know, like and trust. If you want to connect with people you don't know well, be sure to utilize the "list" option they offer. You can choose what those people see, as you wish.

FACEBOOK PAGE

What is it? A business page you can share your business information on as often as you want. If you are an entrepreneur who owns a small service company, like a consulting firm, real estate business, or likewise – a page allows you to share your business with those who want to know about it. You should periodically invite

your "friends" to come over and like your page –
if they are interested in knowing more.

Ideas on what to share: This is the place to
share most of your business updates on
Facebook. Consider sharing blogs you have
created or curated, quotes that speak to your
ideal clients and testimonials from others.

Who should you connect with? People you are
interested in doing business with: past, present,
and future.

FACEBOOK GROUP

What is it? Facebook Groups make it easy to
connect with specific sets of people, like family,
teammates or others who share any of your
Core Four.

Ideas on what to share: Depending on the
purpose of the group you can share many types
of things, including: event/project updates,
photos, blog posts, quotes or documents; and
you can share messages with other group
members.

Who should you connect with? People you share things in common with – industry, type of career, passions, etc.

As an example, one of my passions and the focus of my current business is serving women in business and brands who want to serve them. My desire to connect with and serve women in leadership across the globe inspired me to start a Power Women #PWe3 group on Facebook. It is a place where women can engage, elevate, and empower each other with articles they have read or written, quotes, images, and whatever else is on their hearts to share. The conversations are enlightening and entertaining... and, for the most part, stay focused on solutions with a side of positivity. This group is not directly related to my consulting business or online TV show – however, there are many times I am inspired to write a blog post or pitch a show concept to Kelly based on the conversations sparked in this group. Many of the women in the group have been quoted in the above posts/shows and some of them are reading this right now. (Thank you for your support, #PWe3'ers!)

How can you implement this idea on Facebook?

 Have an idea just not sure how to implement? Tweet me @debra11 and tag #FireMeUp11!

TWITTER

What is it? Is a place to create, learn and share ideas and information instantly, without barriers, or layers of separation between you and those you wish to connect to.

Ideas on what to share: Share your expertise, ask questions and drive traffic to your website or blog posts and those you read. There is a heavy use of hashtags to discover and share on specific topics.

Connections/Audience: Anyone. Friends, peers, leaders, etc... Find new connections whose problems your business solves or who share passions with you. There are private accounts that require you to request approval.

LINKEDIN

What is it? It is an online community where you connect with other professionals. When you join LinkedIn, you get access to people, jobs, news, updates, and insights that help you excel at what you do. You will also strengthen influence in your industry and procure referrals/recommendations.

Ideas on what to share: This is the place to share your business updates. Consider sharing blogs you have created or curated, quotes that speak to your ideal clients, awards and testimonials from others. Always keep your profile freshened up - even while you are currently employed. This practice not only keeps your information up-to-date, it keeps your profile relevant and top of mind with thought-leaders, recruiters, and potential business partners/employers. Finally, if you do not have a blog of your own, but desire to become a thought-leader in your industry, consider publishing posts on LinkedIn.

Who should you connect with? People you want to do business with or would refer business to. Remember, the core concept of LinkedIn is connecting people you know to each other. Ask yourself, would I refer this person to someone else? If the answer is NO – then there is no need to "LINK".

For instance, if they are colleagues who do the same type of work you do, and you would never refer them business - connect with them on Facebook instead.

Now there are two schools of thought on open connecting on LinkedIn. One camp is focused on connecting with anyone and everyone and the other is focused on connecting with people you know or have a strong mutual connection with in real life.

You must choose what works best for you.

GOOGLE+

What is it? G+ is a combination of popular social-media features like comments, photo- and music-sharing, video chat (aka Hangouts), etc. to your social circles. It's basically what any user chooses it to be, from an ongoing conversation to a platform of self-expression, with tools for making it as individual or collective as you want.

Ideas on what to share: Learn new things. Share your expertise. Drive traffic to your website/blog/posts. Host Hangouts - video chats you can record. Increase visibility and search rankings.

Who should you connect with? You can circle anyone on G+ without "sending a friend request".

INSTAGRAM (IG)

What is it? Photo sharing social network. IG is a camera app that also has filters, frames and other basic editing tools... If you love to take photos – this is definitely a network to consider. IG is also a hashtag heavy network.

Ideas on what to share: Your experiences, favorite quotes or images – mostly taken or created by you. There are also several experts who share tips and tricks on infusing IG into your business promo strategy. One key perk to this app – you can take the photo in IG and share it out to multiple social media sites like: Facebook, Twitter, Tumbler, Foursquare, etc.

Who should you connect with? Anyone. You can follow people you know or try searching the hashtags for your Core Four words to see who shares the same interests. Some accounts are private and require you to request the ability to follow them.

PINTEREST

What is it? A place to share your dreams, expertise, and passions with images from the Internet or your personal/purchase photos on your devices. This is a place for you to truly share your story in a very visual way.

Ideas on what to share/pin: Make a board that represents what you value and one for each of your passions, as appropriate. It is ideal to add your favorite quotes, recipes (food or drink), fashion, and home décor style into your board strategy – those are always a hit on Pinterest.

Who should you connect with? Anyone. You can follow people you know or try searching key Core Four words to see who shares the same interests and style. Consider following your industry influencers and clients to keep up on what they are pinning too!

BLOG

What is it? A platform for you to share your thoughts with written word, photos, videos, podcasts, or whatever your heart desires.

Ideas on what to share: Topics that speak to your Core Four. Write a blog about your passions, write posts that solve your ideal clients problems, share your photography on a photo blog... There is no limit to what you can write about on your own blog, however keeping it somewhat focused on a topic is ideal for your followers.

Who should you write for? You will build an audience based on the topics you write about and by consistently driving traffic to your website's blog.

PERSONAL LANDING PAGES

What are they? Personal landing pages (like about.me or follr.com) are ideal for those of you who do not have a website right now or ever desire to have one, but still seek a digital identity online. It is also great for those of you who DO have a website or blog – but want an alternative page to tell your story and drive traffic to your content.

Ideas on what to share: You can share your story and personal descriptor words, add your web links, and include all of your social media accounts so people can get to know YOU! *Here is mine, as an example: debra11.com*

Who should you connect with? You can build an internal community of anyone else who is on the platform!

REVIEW AND DISCOVERY SITES

What are they? Sites like Yelp! and Foursquare/ Swarm allow you to share your passions and community expertise by checking in, leaving tips and recommendations, and sharing your feedback out on other social media streams.

Ideas on what to share: Your favorites in every category from restaurants to theatres. If you are a #Foodie – be sure to check-in when you dine at your favorite restaurants in town, leave a tip or review, share it on social media, and later include a link to it in your profile when you blog about the meal. The same goes for your love of wine, dogs, yoga, hiking, etc.

Who should you connect with?   You can build an internal community of anyone else who is on the platform.   Start by following your friends and add people as you start engaging on one another's tips/tricks/reviews.

Now that you have a general idea of what happens where, choose **one** you do not know much about that sounds interesting to you. Take some time to learn more about it and start adding it to your social media strategy!

#moxiememo

pssst...

When was the last
time you updated
your profile photo?

If people can't recognize
you from your photo,
it's time to change it!

Chapter 8

Taking Your Engagement To 11

"Be brave enough to start conversations that inspire positive change and growth."

- Debra Trappen

Simply put: Online engagement shouldn't be a passive experience.

Rather than waiting for people to reach out to you, proactively engage with others.

Here are some of my all-time favorite tips.

Tip #1: CHOOSE YOUR PROFILE PHOTO WISELY

When was the last time you updated your profile photo across your social media accounts? Can you remember or has it been a LONG time?

MAKE SURE TO CHECK AND CONFIRM IT LOOKS LIKE YOU!

If you have changed your hairstyle or have had SEVERAL birthdays since that photo was taken – update it. NOW. Pretty please.

If you are a 55 years young, newly blonde, brilliant beauty today, don't lose out on meeting a fantastic connection because they were looking for a brunette with curly hair or someone in their 40's! ;)

Seriously now. Having a photo that is 20 years old is NOT a great first impression or positive experience with you. Do you REALLY want someone to meet you for the first time and their first thought to be – "Oh my, she sure looks older in real life!"? I didn't think so.

By the way... this also goes for those overly "photo-shopped" photos!

Last and typed with lots of respect and love – let's talk about pets. I know many people adore their pets. Mine are my little furry loves too. HOWEVER, unless you are planning to send them in your place to network at the party or rock out a business contract negotiation – please make sure your face is your profile pic.   If you want your pooch or kitty in a front and center position – make them your COVER PHOTO instead. Well, everywhere except for LinkedIn... the only people who may consider using pets in their cover photo there are those who work with animals for a living.

So, please jump over to your social profiles (at least Facebook and LinkedIn), confirm your photo is updated, and then PASS THIS ON.

Tip #2: REVIEW YOUR CONTACT INFO

One of the biggest mistakes I see on social networks isn't just WHAT connections post... Shockingly, it is NOT MAKING IT EASY to research and connect from a Facebook (or any social media platform) profile!

Yes. It sounds crazy, but it is true.

I have lost count of how many times I've gone to Facebook to find an email or phone number of an online connection and had to do a web search. Ugh. (Yes, you can send a private message on Facebook, but many people never check that inbox OR the infamous "other" inbox, for that matter!)

If you don't really want to use your main email or mobile number – you can add a general email address and/or a Google Voice number so that people can still reach out to you. Many of the social media sites also give you all sorts of other "contact info" options.

For instance, Facebook allows you add your Twitter and Instagram handles; and offers space to add website links so you can easily share your links to LinkedIn, Blog, Google+, Pinterest, etc... Take a moment and see what others see when they peek at your ABOUT tab.

1. Go to your personal timeline

(mine: facebook.com/debra11)

2. Click the ABOUT tab or add /about to the URL in the address bar

(mine: facebook.com/debra11/about)

3. Follow these directions to see what your page looks like to the public, or anyone else, for that matter! Direct: bit.ly/d11-FB-About

4. Play around with the settings and make sure there is enough information for people to connect with you off of Facebook.

NOW: Repeat this process on all your social media platforms.

Ask yourself: "What is the experience my "Social Media Connections" have if they look up my contact info?"

You will likely find that there are areas you can update...

Tip #3: CHOOSING HANDLES AND HASHTAGS

What is a "handle" and how do you choose it?

Your handle is your online username. It is the "name" you choose to follow the @ on your Twitter or Instagram account or the name you choose to put after / in your custom URL's on sites like Facebook, Pinterest or LinkedIn.

It is ideal if you can secure your full name for your personal accounts and your company name for your business accounts. Even if you do not USE IT, register it just in case you want to in the future.

Have a hard to spell or pronounce name? Choose something easier that speaks to YOU. My affinity for the number 11 is my guide... Whenever possible I secure "debra11" as my username on all platforms – in addition to grabbing "debratrappen" for future use.

NOTE: Please avoid using your "profession" as your main handle. If you choose @GFCupcakeGal and decide to open a wine shop or sell real estate – your handle will not make sense to your new followers. If you want to choose or make a change to your handle, check out: namechk.com to find out where it is still available!

Most important – keep it the same on as many of the platforms as possible. Especially those you choose to use on a consistent basis. This makes it easy for people to remember your handle AND tag you; and that means higher engagement and reach!

 #MoxieMemo: Keeping your social media handles and usernames consistent and simple will elevate your engagement and expand your reach!

What is a hashtag and how do you choose it?

Hashtags are an easy way for people to categorize, find and join conversations on a particular topic. A hashtag is used to highlight keywords or topics within a post, and can be placed anywhere within a post.   Not every single platform uses #hashtags (yet), so please be sure to use them appropriately.

If you are trying to figure out what hashtags you want to use, ask yourself a simple question:

What conversations do I want to spark or join?

Think of #hashtags like your personal brand keywords. If you are passionate about youth justice, gluten-free living, football, or wine - then those are the conversations you want to join in online. Find people talking about those topics by adding a hash/number symbol # in front of the terms, like: #youthjustice, #GFLiving, #NFL, #wine... you get the idea.

Do a little research on similar hashtags being used in those conversations on sites like hashtagify.me – then jump into the social stream with those keyword hashtags and start a conversation.

Tip #4: PROGRESSIVE POWER OF ENGAGEMENT!

This is by far my FAVORITE of all the d11 social media tips and truths. Normally, when I teach this concept in person, I ask people to close their eyes and imagine this scenario. For OBVIOUS reasons, I would love for you to keep yours open and imagine this:

You are out on a walk with friend. You look up and see the most magnificent sunset happening over the lake in your neighborhood. You pull out your phone, snap a few photos and pop it back in your pocket... until you get in your car! You are super excited to share the gorgeous photo you took, so you fluff it up with a filter or frame – and POST IT on a social platform like Facebook, Google+, or Instagram.

THEN YOU WAIT.

What are you waiting for – in this moment? Yes! You are waiting for your first **LIKE** on the photo. When you see it – it feels GOOD, doesn't it? Each like after that brings a smile to your face.

THEN, someone makes a **COMMENT** – maybe something like this: "Gorgeous sunset... Thank you for sharing it!" Oh my goodness, now THAT evokes an even stronger emotion than the like, right? When someone takes the 6 seconds of time to leave that comment – you FEEL SPECIAL.

NOW, imagine you come back in a few hours and see a friend has **SHARED IT** on their timeline! Admit it, you do a little happy dance – even if it is just in your head.

When a friend loves our photo so much they want to share it with their world – that means something special to most of us.

Now, don't forget to engage on the comments people leave on your post. If they took the time to leave thoughts, be sure to **LIKE their comment** (it's like saying "I read this.") and respond back. When you **tag them** in your comment, they know you are talking to them.

 #MoxieMemo: Stop the "post and run" on social media. This behavior is like hosting a cocktail party, decorating the house, opening the front door and then running up to hide in your room all night!

Your mission: DO THIS FOR YOUR FRIENDS!

Be the connection that not only LIKES a post/pic, but comments and shares – when appropriate.

It is a simple way to spread joy on social media AND take your engagement to an 11!

#moxiememo

How do you want to make people feel?

Use the progressive power of social media engagement to inspire smiles!

LIKE * COMMENT * SHARE

Chapter 9

Golden Rule = Give First
Serve + Amplify + Engage

"It takes 20 years to build a reputation and five minutes to ruin it. If you think about that, you'll do things differently."

- Warren Buffet

If you want to amplify your own voice and figure out your focus, I'm going to give you a piece of advice that may see counter productive – at first.

One of the most important things you can do is to follow the golden rule online and "serve, amplify ad engage with others FIRST".

I've been sharing a lot about the importance of finding and nourishing YOU -- YOUR values, passions and purpose.   While it is key to know who you are – from the inside out - it doesn't stop there.

When you go out into the world, even (or maybe especially!) in the virtual world, you have to find your place in an already-established conversation.   Most people know the big influencers and tastemakers in their industry or areas of interest. If you want to make a place for yourself, you're going to need to do some work introducing yourself.

Have you ever met a child who is super smart and likes to show off his or her brilliance? Yes, it is cute... for a bit.   Then, frankly, it can be overwhelming and annoying. Adults tend to put up with it from children; and hope they grow out of it! However, for adults, it is not acceptable to gratuitously talk about yourself, your achievements, your message... or make your posts all about YOU YOU YOU!

Using social media platforms as a megaphone for your "ME" message is irritating, harmful to your mission to connect with people and damaging to your online reputation. One of the worst things for your personal brand (or your business/career) is to get a reputation as someone who just blathers on, posts only about him/herself and doesn't pay attention to what anyone else is saying.

You will grow and nurture a better reputation by participating respectfully on blogs and in social media conversations. Focus on sharing your connection's tweets, pins, and social updates. You don't have to be a wallflower. When you are your fabulous, friendly, passionate self it does two things. First, it establishes you as a thoughtful person who is generous, fun to connect with, and interested in learning from others.

Secondly, this behavior also helps establish you as a go-to person in your field or industry. You are not being friendly and sharing others' tweets and statuses, you're also becoming a curator of what's new and interesting. People will start to follow you because of your ability to roundup the best of what's happening in your industry.

Meet Lisa Archer, CEO of Live Love Homes and Co-Founder of The Geeky Girls. Lisa exemplifies the concept of GIVE FIRST. If you follow her on social media – you can't miss her LOVE for and commitment to the communities she serves. I asked her to share one of her "giving adventures" and she, of course, was happy to share.

Here is her story:

"At Live Love Charlotte we have launched a division where we give back to our military called Live Love Veterans - in 2013. The first year we had our event where we honored our Veterans at a Carolina Panthers Monday night football game with a tailgate. We also had a canned food drive. In 2014, we had an Angel tree where we collected over 50 gift cards for our disabled Veterans and their families. It has been such a blessing and an honor to love on those that have sacrificed so much."

KEY SOCIAL PLATFORM TIPS:

1. **Facebook:** Set up FRIEND LISTS and an INTEREST LIST of the influencer business pages you want to listen to. Be sure to check the lists a few times a week, use the progressive power of engagement (Like, Comment, Share) and amplify their message throughout the year.

2. **Twitter:** Set up TWITTER LISTS with the specific connections you want to listen to. Check the lists a few times a week, engage with them and retweet the tweets that resonate with you. If you make your list public, the person will know they have been added to your list and that can trigger another opportunity to connect with them. Remember to create a few lists. Start with one that wrangles the influencers in your business/industry and another to keep up with others who share your personal passions and interests.

   Also, strive to have 40-50% of your tweets a combination of retweets (RT) or replies (@ is the first symbol in your tweet). This shows you share, engage AND listen!

3. **LinkedIn:** TAGGING is so underutilized on LinkedIn and it is such a great way to filter your connections. Tag the connections you want to give attention to. Put an appointment on your calendar to check in on your LinkedIn connections to keep up to date on their careers and stay top of mind with them.

8 UNIVERSAL LIST CATEGORIES:

To keep things uniform across your social channels, use the same categories for your lists and tags.

1. A+ Champions: A "go to" list of people who don't let you down
2. Personal Friends: People you have met in person
3. Framily: Friends & family you share the most with
4. Clients: People you have or are doing business with
5. Prospects: People you want to do business with
6. Collaborators: People you want to collaborate with
7. Competition: People doing similar work
8. Influencers: People you want to watch to learn from

Chapter 10

Keys To Amplify Your Voice

"As you prepare your content for each social channel, do not over-think your posts. Keep them short, sweet and easy to SHARE!"

- Rebekah Radice

You've worked diligently on becoming part of the content-sharing community, added value to (and sprinkled the progressive power philosophy in) social media conversations, commented on blogs and participated in many thought-provoking chats along the way.

At the same time, you have to think about positioning yourself as a knowledgeable member of the industry with the blog posts YOU produce. Creating and sharing content that represents your Core Four, industry, and hot topics will promote engagement, provoke debate, attract ideal connections and inspire shares!

Now it's time to work on amplifying YOUR voice.

Here are 5 keys to making this happen:

Key #1: Create a content calendar and promotion strategy

Put together 22 topics you want to blog about in the next 12 months. These should be topics you are passionate about, answer problems you/your business solve, etc. To start, schedule out time to write a blog post for each topic, then create a short video message, haikudeck.com presentation, and/or design a fun visual meme/quote to share for each post with programs like canva.com or PicMonkey.

This will create at least one piece of custom content every single week with your point of view attached to it. 22 blogs turn into 66 or 88 pieces of sharable content. You can do it all in one week, quarterly, or monthly... however, the farther in advance you create the content – the better. 20% of your content time should be spent creating the content... 80% should be promoting it!

Key #2: Add social follow and share buttons on your website/materials.

MAKE IT EASY for your audience to share and connect with you online. Include social calls-to-action that show people where they can find you on social media. Also install plugins on your blog that allow your audience to share your content, and/or opt in to follow your blog RSS feed. Make sure this info is everywhere from your home page and your blog posts, to your email marketing messages and printed collateral at trade shows.

Key #3: Customize your message based on the platform.

While you're creating and sharing fabulous content, think of WHEN you're putting it up and how it looks. For the love of all things social media – PLEASE use the right language on each platform... and stop the generic auto-posting! Each social media platform has a preferred "style" and better times to put your posts out there. Analyze your social media analytics to find out when you should be posting and how to optimize for maximum shares. (Not sure how to figure this out? Just pop on Google or Bing and search "when is the best time to post on _____?" There are plenty of experts who can guide you through this!)

Bottom line: Treat each piece of content according to where it is going so it resonates with that specific audience. The more custom you make it, the more likely to spread. For example:

Facebook audiences are mainly people who know, like and trust you, the length of posts permitted allows space to share your thoughts – at length and visual posts with photos and videos get fantastic engagement. Hashtags are lightly used and URL's don't require a www. or http:// to perform.

Google+ is similar to Facebook, however it also allows you to format with bold and italics, is hashtag heavy, and sharing photos and videos is the preferred format for most of your audience.

Twitter requires you to be short and sweet. If you want people to share (retweet) your tweet – keep your characters to 111 or less! Also, you can and should let your sass and sizzle shine. You need to attract attention in seconds. Hashtags and links are heavily used and URL's don't require a www. or http:// to perform.

LinkedIn is a place for you to shine your knowledge so instead of cutting/pasting a mere link to the content, use the ample character allotment and give YOUR point of view on the post. As mentioned in chapter 7, you can also publish your own posts here to really get your point of view across.

Key #4: Implement a guest blogging program.

Put together a list of 6-11 bloggers you love to read, share and who also compliment your message. Message them to find out if they would be interested in being part of your guest blogging program. It could be as simple as you each write 2 blog posts for each other in the upcoming 12 months and commit to a simple, minimum social media promotion strategy.

If you put together a team of 6 bloggers – that is another 12 pieces of fresh content on your blogs and tons of conversation in your social streams.

Key #5: Interview Industry Influencers

Embracing change, leveraging social media, and truly leading by example starts with interviews. (The next one will be published on Friday this week, so stay tuned!)

Consider interviewing one of two ways:

Schedule A G+ Hangout/Skype To Do A LIVE Interview: Be sure to have your questions prepared ahead of time to show respect for their time. This option is great when you have never met the person in real life. You will "virtually" get a flavor for who they are and, of course, be able to connect a bit more "face to face"! Do your best to schedule a video chat, however, if you must do a phone interview, go for it.

Email Your List of Questions - This option is great if you know the person or they have a wickedly wonky schedule since it allows them to answer the questions whenever they are available.

Once you have the blog post or interview answers together, here are some tips:

- Format the posts the same way —every time. Your audience will start to recognize and look for them.
- Create a special hashtag for those posts so that you can easily track them online. Include it in the post title.
- Don't assume interviewees will promote their post and then get disappointed when they don't.
  - *ASK them to assist you in promoting it to their community.*
  - *Be sure to tag them when YOU promote the post. Getting it on their radar, in this manner, nearly guarantees they will amplify it to their community!*

The best way to amplify your voice and grow your online audience is by fostering a connected, engaged community.

The more your entire follower-base collaborates and connects "in the stream", the more exposure your voice and social presence receives. Not only that, when you consider how most social media platform's algorithms work, the posts that receive the most engagement receive the most exposure in the main feed. When you create content your audience is inspired to engage on AND you personally spark and continue the conversation online you amplify your messages and, ultimately, your voice!

 #MoxieMemo: If you want others to help you amplify your voice, make your messages worthy of sharing. Be different. **Stand out from the crowd.** Be YOU!

Entrepreneur side note: Because of the importance of social media, its intricacies, and the time commitment necessary to make good use of it, hiring someone to be your brand's social media manager can be a great investment if you find you just can't be consistent on your own. You should be in charge of your personal social media posts or engagement, however hiring someone to help you blog (in your voice) and keep your stream filled your content - new and repurposed posts - is an excellent option for the busy entrepreneur.

Want to chat about these tips? Tweet me @debra11 and include the hashtag **#FireMeUp11!**

Coffee in my mug.
Big girl panties on.
Swing in my step.
Smile on my face.
Twinkle in my eye.
Glitter on my lips.
Sparkle in my wand.
Moxie mission accepted.
Watch out world...
HERE. I. COME.

~Debra Trappen
dllconsulting.com

Chapter 11

Flourish with Focus

"What you focus on flourishes."

- Debra Trappen

There is a lot to do when you are defining a brand and niche for yourself and your business. It is easy to get overwhelmed by it all and think you have to magically morph into a magnificent, magnetic multi-tasker.

(Say that 11 times fast!)

STOP.

Take a deep breath. In fact, stop multi-tasking all together. Yes, I said it (well, typed it). Don't multi-task.

Don't try to do it all. You can't.

At most you'll do a bunch of stuff in an unexceptional, ordinary way.

In order to move from mediocre existence to a **FIRED UP,** flourishing life and business - **you must focus on your priorities.**

F-O-C-U-S and implement
one thing at a time!

Flourishing means prioritizing, pursuing and experiencing a fired up life; it's about building and nurturing your relationships, enjoying what you have, striving to fulfill your purpose and reaching your potential.

If everything is a priority, then nothing really is.

Maintain your focus and be consistent. This will help you share your story, gain influence, nurture relationships, build a successful brand and ultimately serve and care for the people who are looking for you!

Tips & Truths to keep you on track:

- Take time to revisit your Core Four and focus on developing and nurturing yourself to 11.
- Print out your WORDS and post them on your bathroom mirror, on your closet door, at your desk, in the laundry room...
- Be intentional about your social media presence and engage, elevate, empower and entertain others while sharing your Core Four.
- Take time to turn off your technology and focus on planning, implementing, assessing, pivoting, and taking your plans to 11.
- Take time to craft magnificent, magnetic relationships and focus on being present, honoring your loved ones, and elevating your relationships to an 11.
- Implement what you have learned in this book and FOCUS on the elements of your signature formula for flourishing - your business and LIFE will go to 11.

- ## YOU ARE WORTH IT.

BE GOOD TO EACH OTHER
THINK BEFORE YOU SPEAK
PRAY FOR CLARITY

STOP JUDGING, START EMBRACING
HELP A FRIEND GET
CLOSER TO THEIR DREAM
SMILE AND LAUGH OFTEN

SPRINKLE LOVE

dllconsulting.com

Wrapping It UP!

It was my heart's desire to share tips, tricks and truths with you to guide and inspire you into your greatness, get you out of your own way, and ignite your soul to confidently go after your dreams fearlessly, fiercely, and with a fire that sparks everyone around you.

To end our time together, I thought it would be fun to share some of my favorite mantras and memes. These words surround me – on my walls, mirrors, fridge, phone, laptop and beyond! You will also find them on my Pinterest boards!

 Let me know which ones resonate the most with you by tweeting me @debra11 and, as always, please use the hashtag **#FireMeUp11!**

YOU MAY BE ABLE TO FAKE SMARTS, ATTITUDE OR EXPERIENCE ONLINE. YOU CAN'T FAKE CONSISTENCY. DO THE WORK!

@debrall

repeat after me...
Today is going to
be a magnificent day!
DIVINE things
are going to
happen to
and for me.
It is my
time to
SHINE.
The best is
still to come!

dllconsulting.com

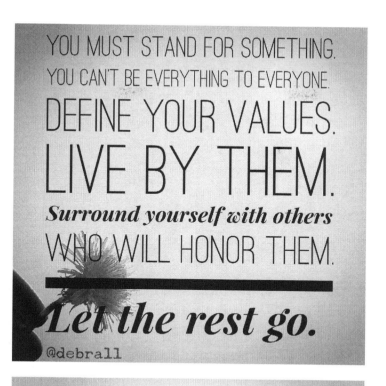

YOU MUST STAND FOR SOMETHING.
YOU CAN'T BE EVERYTHING TO EVERYONE.

DEFINE YOUR VALUES.
LIVE BY THEM.

Surround yourself with others

WHO WILL HONOR THEM.

Let the rest go.

@debrall

Not everyone is going to
want, like, accept
or know how to receive
your energy.
Make peace with
that & keep on
sprinkling
your Magic.

@debrall

CONNECT WITH DEBRA

WEBSITE
d11consulting.com

FACEBOOK PAGE
facebook.com/d11consulting

FACEBOOK PROFILE
facebook.com/debra11

TWITTER
twitter.com/debra11

PINTEREST
pinterest.com/debra11

GOOGLE +
plus.google.com/u/0/+debratrappen

YOUTUBE
youtube.com/user/debratrappen

INSTAGRAM
instagram.com/debra11

ABOUT.ME
about.me/debra11

TUMBLR
debra11.tumblr.com

SLIDESHARE
slideshare.net/debra11

Additional PRAISE...

"Debra is the master and asking questions and truly getting to the bottom of things like values, mission and niche so that you can create something truly unique to you. When you work with Debra, you realize that no matter what industry you are in and how crowded it might feel, you have your own unique set of gifts and talents that allow you to succeed and set yourself apart. Debra is masterful at helping people shift from fear and competition to embracing who they are and building on that from a place of abundance."

- Nicole Mangina
Nicole Mangina Inc, Real Estate Agent and Business Mentor

"During the short time I shared with Debra she took my passion, my wife's passion and our businesses to 11! I now have more business just from the life changing words she shared. What Debra offers isn't just great material, but a lifetime of amazing life changing tips that will take your success and business to 11."

- Brandon Couch
CEO/Founder of BC Creative Media Marketing Solutions

"Debra has helped me face some major growth spurts in my business life and personal life. She was able to show me ways to use the changes I was going through to make positive decisions that would help me accept the growth I was facing. It was overwhelming and I tend to shy away from taking compliments about things I'm doing. She taught me to embrace that with more grace. Debra is a gift. She listens intently to help walk you through to realize the answers you were seeking. She helps you find your strengths and how to deal with any weaknesses. Debra is filled with compassion and no holds barred truth telling. She isn't telling you what you want to hear but telling you what you need to hear."

- Rosemary Buerger
ERA Strother Real Estate Broker Associate

GETTING FIRED UP! WITH DEBRA

A dynamic, professional educator and speaker, Debra Trappen fires up entrepreneurs & growth-minded organizations on a regular basis, focused on igniting and empowering women in business. Her more than 11,000+ hours of live, energetic and inspiring speaking, training, video, and webinar sessions are evident as she captivates audiences. Debra's professional media training (CooperKatz) and performances as an actor and vocalist from a young age have enabled her to perfect trainings and workshops that carry wide appeal.

Debra offers training through her Fire Up Your Personal Brand Workshop, a custom, 6-hour experience designed to inspire, ignite, and generally kick BOOST entrepreneurs and corporate teams into HIGH GEAR through individual and group consulting.

Debra Trappen also offers personal and small group personal branding sessions for executives and leaders, helping each to solidify their Core Four: values, passions, purpose and niche. Debra counsels use of a simple, focused social media "storytelling-style" strategy, designed to engage and serve current connections, build deeper relationships, attract ideal clients and build a life and business that FIRES YOU UP!

Interested in bringing Debra to your next event or conference?

Schedule a discovery chat to uncover the possibilities!

Online Calendar
d11consulting.com/schedule

Email
pssst@d11consulting.com

WORKSHEETS & RESOURCES

Core Values Exercise Teaser
Value Words A-D:

- Abundance
- Acceptance
- Accessibility
- Accomplishment
- Accountability
- Accuracy
- Achievement
- Acknowledgement
- Activeness
- Adaptability
- Adoration
- Adroitness
- Advancement
- Adventure
- Aesthetics
- Affection
- Affluence
- Aggressiveness
- Agility
- Alertness
- Altruism
- Amazement
- Ambition
- Amusement
- Anticipation
- Appreciation
- Approachability
- Approval
- Art
- Articulacy
- Artistry
- Assertiveness
- Assurance
- Attentiveness
- Attractiveness
- Audacity
- Authenticity
- Availability
- Awareness
- Awe
- Balance
- Beauty
- Being the best
- Belonging

- Benevolence
- Bliss
- Boldness
- Bravery
- Brilliance
- Buoyancy
- Calmness
- Candor
- Capability
- Care
- Carefulness
- Celebrity
- Certainty
- Challenge
- Change
- Charity
- Charm
- Chastity
- Cheerfulness
- Clarity
- Cleanliness
- Clear-mindedness
- Cleverness
- Closeness
- Comfort
- Commitment
- Community
- Compassion
- Competence
- Competition
- Completion
- Composure
- Concentration
- Confidence
- Conformity
- Congruency
- Connection
- Consciousness
- Conservation
- Consistency
- Contentment
- Continuity
- Contribution
- Control

- Conviction
- Conviviality
- Coolness
- Cooperation
- Cordiality
- Correctness
- Country
- Courage
- Courtesy
- Craftiness
- Creativity
- Credibility
- Cunning
- Curiosity
- Daring
- Decisiveness
- Deference
- Delight
- Dependability
- Depth
- Desire
- Determination
- Devotion
- Devoutness
- Dexterity
- Dignity
- Diligence
- Direction
- Directness
- Discipline
- Discovery
- Discretion
- Diversity
- Dominance
- Dreaming
- Drive
- Duty
- Dynamism
- ...

Directions and E-Z words:
firemeup11.com/ValuesExercise

11 CORE VALUE WORDS

1. _____

2. _____

3. _____

4. _____

5. _____

6. _____

7. _____

8. _____

9. _____

10. _____

11. _____

Surround yourself with excellence and those
aligned with your values + goals!

Soul Tank Inventory NOTES:

_____

_____

_____

_____

_____

_____

_____

_____

_____

_____

Purpose Exercise NOTES:

Niche Statement NOTES:

pssst... Smile when you wake up.

seize & savor each moment.

Give Yourself Grace

BE Fierce. Feisty. Fabulous.

FEARLESS.

e m b r a c e c h a n g e

sprinkle blessings & encouragement

NOW is the time. THIS is the place.

You are the one.

@debrall * dllconsulting.com

Made in the USA
Charleston, SC
27 July 2015